T0208506

Trapped in a Bosque

SHERIDAN BROWN

authorHOUSE®

AuthorHouse™
1663 Liberty Drive
Bloomington, IN 47403
www.authorhouse.com
Phone: 833-262-8899

Published by AuthorHouse 03/15/2023

ISBN: 979-8-8230-0126-7 (sc)
ISBN: 979-8-8230-0127-4 (e)

Library of Congress Control Number: 2023903457

Print information available on the last page.

Cover Painting: Dyad, 2019, Robert Gunderman

This book is printed on acid-free paper.

Contents

Trapped in a Bosque

Body Armor

for M and H

Vespers

Vespers

Coping with simulated life
a sanitarium guest in a Swiss retreat
a splash of bitters in my matcha tea

Bond with support dogs in neon vests
read letters returned address unknown
shoot videos of lisping dorgies
bake grain-free noodles
curate a garden of weeds

Anything to not be me
a glass half empty you're a fool
half full delusional

A devil's inside the door
in a silly red suit, wrapping his claws
around my fear

Learning to be humble
shedding the weight of things
I become executor of my life

A prayer room welcomes
whispering soothing chants
I take a step toward heaven lite
forgetting seasons in hell.

I Dreamt I Died Last Night

I dreamt I died last night
and woke up feeling free
making a list of everything I didn't need

Laying a tarp on the smooth espresso floor
piles sprang to life sharing a common goal.

First heavy items

ceramic pans for a family of five
jumbo towels queen-size sheets
unused glasses custom etched

worn-out Nikes empty silken garment bags
expired sunscreen eco-friendly potpourri
books reminders of bad choices
verboten Madame Bovary

Mounding a structure
connecting landscapes yet unseen
a close encounter of the fifth kind
with my alien self.

Cue the Tumbrels

Cue the tumbrels, cut the mics
A moment of silence for all opinions

Wherever my soul is
it needs a Kevlar vest to shield
its delicate membrane.

Exquisite soundlessness
is surprisingly welcome.

Touché Cliché

When push comes to shove you lie straight face
truth be told it's hard to see forest from trees
With heartfelt thanks I fall hook line and sinker
wrapping my wrists with a ribbon of words
for wearing my heart on my sleeve
Imagine fragile Brussels lace
shielding my face from your gaze.

R v. W

The mold grew in dark places left to its own
devices
Imposters laughing in the doorway they owned
for now

Our eyes darting in the corner for a sliver of light
to frame an exit

It's unconfirmed who sounded the ding ding ding
in the fog of war.

Timed Out

Living in a failing state

  you can rate

    fake cheer craft beer

      pinched nerves saboteurs

        wide moats false hopes

          rolling blackouts trolling dropouts

         dying news whack crews

          Bosch hats market stats

Front row to history.

When

can is must I see struggle share terror do nothing

silent as a full-blown butterfly
admired for dying gracefully
animals we loved and used
communal haze.

Tell me a story what you wanted what you got

Leave me to mourning my ill-spent tropes
mumbling to myself.

It is Written

Where does it say poems should be
about soufflés and crinolines
dismembered body parts and skin
mollusks and tides, bruised fruit, troubled dreams,
hallways leading nowhere?

Mine are lies about lies.

I live in Geppetto's cottage
a suspect in a makeshift prison under house arrest
Cooing doves in the eaves soothe my lying self
with ease
No reason to concede my faults and be released.

The Ecstasy of Saint Theresa

Standing before Bernini's sculpture

in its darkened chapel

I become a supplicant in a hooded robe

feeling insubstantial vertigo confusion

Label it Stendahl Syndrome neatly wrapped

or social media app

Shaking shivering mouthing guttural noises

help me understand how beauty

transforms malady into poetry.

Pavane for Older Women

Pavane for Older Women 1

We are the discarded diviners
the redoubt against cruel insiders

dismissing the duping delight of the smirk
giving away the unintended alert

We see you now without illusion
casting our past to its rightful conclusion

no safe journey for memories like stones
the souls of the dead under piles of bones.

The Sensitive

Her spirit guides were animals
not the cunning monkey king the reckless tiger
or ruthless rat
She chose a loping dog to worship easily.

No mushrooms no witches brew
on the verge of understanding nothing
the gates of perception opened.

Pavane for Older Women 2

I passed a storybook cottage
a mini turret above the door
blurry glass windows with uncanny light
an overgrown garden without a view.

Did Norma Shearer live here
dreams of impossible fame
marcelled hair, phony Brit accent
slinky satin gowns with no underwear

Toward the end she couldn't recall
whose Oscar it was in her little room
in a home where aging actors go
greeting strangers she once knew.

Greta G and Mrs. R

Garbo's later life watching bad tv
walking aimlessly going to bed early
The word fun I don't recognize
she may have said.

Mrs. Robinson filled with rage
her dreams wasted on a suburban stage
Sex was her weapon, her talent filled with malice
plotting to make vengeance her primary solace.

On the worn out road to Damascus
a harried pilgrim pines for second chances
foraging for feverfew to calm
those low slung dreams.

Pavane for Older Women 3

She woke up in her old sedan
Thanksgiving Day a trying time in any case
the back seat a ziggurat of plastic baskets
a snoozing dog curled on a comforter of lace

She let the notices gather on her door
after her birthday didn't care anymore
A sheriff showed up she was ready for the news
of what to take and what to lose

Remembering if you sleep in your car
find a Target lot and park not far
from the acid yellow lamps.

The moment in free fall felt like a sigh
once purposeful and kind somewhere
she accidentally lost her mind.

Pavane for Older Women 4

She was living on the street for years,
never sleeping through the night,
most of her teeth were gone

The cowboy hat covering bald spots,
shielding leathery skin a ranch in Kansas
someone else's childhood.

Heavy rings on every finger
silver serpents crescent moons evil eyes,
glued-on nails replacing manicures so long ago.

If there is such a thing as luck a room came up.
Placing a mattress in a corner on the floor
where she could watch the door,
a private bathroom and space to cook soft food.

With colored pencils she drew memories
dogs she walked unreliable boyfriends
cars that wouldn't start the slow slide down
Terror of the past was less but not the loss.

Pavane for Older Women 5

Undesirable unwanted
worth more dead than alive
she crawls into a body bag
zipping from the inside

Seconal in applesauce
scarves tied to door knobs
a frosty night the motor runs
warming a closed garage

A Tarantella dancer spins
eluding a hairy spider

A warrior crone too old for battle
spares acolytes their pain

A lioness spoons her cubs in her lair
giving wisdom another chance.

In the Tarot

In the Tarot the Queen of Swords is the Crone
the Dragonfly brings change

What's left of life's small pleasures
is calling in the chips
I may not be a cartomancer
but know when my hand is played out.

As Queen of Swords
I checked my options at the door
transformed for a splice of time into
the Dragonfly

Eyes sewn shut no vertigo
no parallactic view it felt eternal.

A Canticle

A witness to my own demise
I can't remember why I went upstairs
or comprehend a distance or a size.

A callous druid distorts my sight
spinning a filmy veil my body a ruin
a monument to decay.

This hapless prayer's a yearning
to stop time where there is no sound
only searing light in a liminal space
between release and nothing.

The Brink

The loss was a near death moment

floating in blackness

separated from myself

in soundlessness

no stars

no air

no wanting

no feeling

Relief.

Infinite Loop

Brandishing a weapon on myself
I jump into a den of screaming jackals
following their nature to leave no flesh behind

I wear a custom hair shirt (self-denial comes in many forms)
a grape for lunch a barefoot walk in icy snow
a toxic hour with a miscreant

Infinite loops programmed to never end
unless poetic justice intervenes.

The Mask

The bronze a fractured face with emptied eyes
poised to enthrall
veiled to seduce
a death mask freezing last moments.

Reptiles shed their skin
to transform and beguile
a tic becomes a tremor
my lizard brain whispers its intent.

Rahu

I am

the handmaid of grift

the undoer of good deeds

the engineer of whirlwinds

the maker of sorrows

the titan of worthless whims

the gambler intent on zero

I am Rahu

steeped in illusion.

What Would Sylvia Do?

Not the best role model to make suffering your goal

less of it and be a ghost

more of it and score devotion

plot the end and set in motion undone dreams

Do I dare to eat a peach or let fear reign supreme.

The Relic

In the dream I am folded
into a metal box
filigreed full of holes
enclosed by a pointed metal roof

Shrinking skin gravelly voice
shivering and damp
struggling to sit upright
there must be some mistake

Neither martyr nor saint the walls fall away
with a tinny sound I'm awake.

Trapped in
a Bosque

Trapped in a Bosque

Trapped in a bosque you caught me unaware
ensnared by your careful affection.

Surrounded by a web of tendrils light comes
through
I start to feel my way but fail to notice thorns

Like a helpless badger the teeth of the torture
machine
bloody with hair and bone

scratches start to swell hard to tell
if I emerge whole.

Tunnel of Love

Sidereal time slowed
to full stop.
A funhouse ride in a jerky car
keeping me safe with a clammy metal bar
from falling into the shadowy murk
that covers the rail
It guided me out of the silence and dark
into a deconstructed pale
leaving me trapped in my own darkness.

A Fine Romance

The blue-black wave rushed up to me
and back again I chased the taunting rhythm
the frisson of the foam
Catch me if you can it whispered let's play
and so I did surrendering to the power
with buckled knees
Take me away do as you please
You are my romantic lead.

Aviary

I can't undo my disrepair
with no game left to play
slipping back to old routines
swaying on a wooden swing
in an open cage
a toy bird with manicured wings
losing her song her curiosity
dissolves into a swirl of feathers.

Weather Systems

I feel a riptide when you are next to me
an aura coats you like Giotto's saints
expressionless flat golden

Floating aimlessly waiting for the undertow
powerless to swim away
pull pull pull
my flapping arms surrender to weightlessness
stopping time.

Firestarter

Molten lava follows the sluice
beauty destroying itself Disruptor!
A Grand Guignol Burn down the house
remnants leave an acrid smell
a chalky taste on the tongue
The Phoenix a Dodo bird
no ashes to rise from.

There Was a Moment

There was a moment when everything changed
a faint breath a flicker of your attention
of letting down your guard

at that instant I understood
your eyes said disappear

Admitting what was there from the start
I let myself break my own heart.

In a Star Chamber

In a star chamber of my own design
willingly I go resigned to the ninth circle
where treachery is the clarion call

Taking a moment to assess the scene
Kubrick would approve
banal, luxe, slippers for the granite floor

no doors of course
forever home.

String Quartet

Giving lip service to pretend
while waiting for a better ending
dislocated on a thin tether
I'm playing in the Auschwitz String Quartet.

Blaring horns glaring lights
the prison stripes merged with my skin
barbed wire cuts my fingers
burn performing sad sonatas

Slowly with a jagged trowel
carefully moving the hardened soil
I carve a tunnel to somewhere.

The Narcissist

Vengeance was her talent, a revanchist at heart,
she strode into a room like the Anschluss had begun,
taking back lost territory, the invader's purpose to demean.
Her therapist called her scary and that was being kind.
Plotting to reclaim at any cost what she believed was hers,
her presence was the opposite of sparking joy.
Do sorcerers make house calls to conjure up an herbal brew
strong enough to exorcise the pain she brings?
Her greatest pleasure.

Unforced Errors

Tricked by charlatans with promises of louche cabals
my powers for predicting pain elude me once again

There is no learning from my mistakes
Opportunities slither by in seductive guises
ending in a poisoned bite of unforced errors.

If angels don't have wings and walk among us
I'd ask them for advice on how to spot the demons
who don't breathe fire or have a sulfur scent

Instead are full of treacheries and charm
with schemes and plots to harm their waiting prey.

Body Armor

Body Armor

A chem trail fading in a sober sky
an armadillo's shadow on the sand
a bee on its back
the intention of a shiny black crow
the blank screen whispering secrets

Savonarola's ashes scattering
The chattering Rialto in flames.

Abattoir

Waiting to be lifted off
the meat hook legs dangle
flailing importune

Feeling no recourse
mind maze shut down
until further notice

Still as hunted pangolins
frozen in dissolving time
on high alert no rescue

Reaching up to pull away
whoosh ripped raw
sticky flesh gives urgency

Undazzled by hopes and prayers
Forcing random adverbs into breath.

Tuesday 2pm

Through the glass I watch the rain-soaked leaves

   cling to a brittle tree like an aging virus

    suddenly they let go becoming a whirling dervish

    the shambolic circle disappearing into dark water.

Dark Optics

Besotted by dark matter

clusters of stars act on their own behalf

gravity be damned

In the future, images will only exist in the mind

reality be damned

Cold comfort feeling so small

There is no time at all.

Starry Night

The cypress trees outside my window

block the view

Maligned by Vincent they sway

stately

evergreen

not a grim reminder

A portal to something else.

Folly Garden

After the rain I checked the Folly Garden
so lush and green it hurt my eyes

Mapping pathways already known
no change among the ruins some misplaced
rocks.

The Temple of Piety columns of paper mache'
The Sunken Pond two black swans glide by
The Pyramid no hidden vault inside

The Milkmaid silver buckled three inch heels
braided queue embossed satin decolleté
perfectly prepared to court disaster

Passing the hired Hermit clothed in hemp
crouched before the Grotto overgrown with moss
his toenails painted blue contrasting matted hair

Reading Rousseau blank pages though,
he guards the cave secrets safe
the trickery of artifice a feeling

Still there's power in the sense of place
gathering twisted branches
I make a fragile altar to the absent gods.

Biography

Sheridan Brown was born in the Midwest and graduated from the University of Michigan.

She has been a high school teacher, a fashion and media journalist for international publications, a licensed cognitive behavioral psychotherapist in private practice, an advocate for animals-chimpanzees from labs, farm animals, senior dogs and a supporter of the contemporary art community. She lives in Los Angeles.

Printed in the United States
by Baker & Taylor Publisher Services